Heal My Heart O Lord

Heal My Heart O Lord

JOAN HUTSON

Ave Maria Press
Notre Dame, Indiana 46556

Library of Congress Catalog Card No: 75-30493
International Standard Book Number: 0-87793-106-2 (paper)
0-87793-107-0 (cloth)

Contents

Born Heart...

Before you were born, you felt the shattering
tensions around you in the sheltering womb of your
mother. You stirred with unrest as forceful currents
in the world you had not yet entered, entered you.

Words you did not understand taught you love, and
hate; peace and turmoil, security and insecurity.
The protection of your mother's body could not
insulate you from the feelings she experienced.
If she did not want you, you trembled with this awesome truth; if she was overjoyed with the expectancy
of you, you felt reached for; you felt the mantle of
love wrapped around you.

Then in that moment of your birth . . . if reluctant
arms accepted you, your heart became an apology.
If eager arms reached out for you, your heart became
an instant alleluia! In between this latitude of
welcome, all are born.

Some will never know warmth; some will never
know cold. Some will hear My name every day in
prayer; some will hear My name every day in curses.
Some will breathe in hate with every breath; some will
breathe in love with every breath. Circumstances over
which you had no control formed you, reformed you,

made you regress, made you progress, made you reach out, made you draw back into yourself.

Your days as a small child are too complicated for you to remember. I, your Creator, see the ways circumstances crippled you. I haven't forgotten one joy or one sorrow that you experienced. I know how these joys and sorrows have reached down through all the years of your life, freeing you, or binding you, making your heart sing, or making your heart cry. I know the healing that your life-tossed child soul needs. I can loose the tethers and free you from all that began to bind you from the moment you were conceived . . . for you were conceived from My heart . . . in My heart, and of My heart.

With a father's love let Me dissolve all that binds you . . . let Me set you free! Let Me loosen the grips of crippling experiences. C

Child Heart...

It took courage for your child heart to reach out to the world. If only you could have been surrounded with love and understanding until you better knew how to cope with misunderstanding. If only your hands could have been filled as you reached out. But worse than remaining empty, often their needs were not even recognized. So the hands were withdrawn secretly and quickly to avoid awkward moments.

How many times you were short-circuited when you so desperately needed to feel the flow of the human circuit. Each time you worked out your defenses. Slowly you learned not to reach so far. So much could happen to your outstretched, searching fingers. People too preoccupied to listen dismissed you without understanding. Smiles you intended to give were retracted; words you intended to say were swallowed; thoughts you intended to share were dissipated.

Unfeeling parents, teachers and friends closed more and more doors in your face. You struggled to be yourself in a world that really didn't care what your self was. Your successes and defeats blended together because no one was interested in either one.

You were shaped and destroyed by those who loved you and those who refused to love you; by those who always asked more than you had to give; by those who saw nothing even when you gave your all; by those who didn't care if you gave anything.

I've kept all these misfortunes in My heart, and I understand how you were crippled by them. I know you are not free today because of them. I purchased freedom for you, and I'm waiting to regive it in its fullness. I know what needs remembering, I know what needs forgetting, trust Me to heal your child-hurts now. Place your heart in My hands. I will touch it to wholeness! ♡

Adolescent Heart...

How many of My people were scarred during the vulnerable years of growing up. You, who had so many hopes for your place in the world, found it difficult to find "a place in the sun." In breathless anticipation you explained your visions. As clear as they were in your mind, they began to come out of focus as they were minimized by practical minds.

You couldn't always accept the life goals others had; you did hear a different drummer. For many of you, the beat grew fainter and fainter, and in the end your step faltered, stumbled, because the world silenced your drummer. Some of you rebelled and beat your own drums and others followed you. Some of you lost the spirit of walking anywhere and waited listening . . . listening for someone to start beating, for something to set the tempo.

You reached out, young hearts, to embrace the world, to remake the world, to convert the world to what you believed to be better. You weren't counting costs; you were committed. But the immovable masses are complacent, not liking life as it was, but enduring it; not inflamed with life, but watching embers die. Slowly, your visions vanished, and you, defeatingly, took your place in the ranks of superficial living, living a life you truly did not believe in. Your voice was stilled. It became easier to let the stones cry out. And now you blame yourself for a life you are not dedicated to. . . .

Instead of censuring yourself let My healing light disclose for you tremendous opportunities lying dormant around you, waiting to be discovered and activated. It really doesn't matter what you are doing in My world! It matters "why." Do what you do, because of Me. . . . I said, "Pay the last even as the first." Though you have come to Me late . . . after you have suffered all the throes of growing up . . . I, who have seen you try to grow, will bless you now with an understanding of what you can do now to live as fully as possible in the place your world has let you be.

C

Disappointed Heart...

You will always hunger and you will always thirst.
For what would satisfy you, this world can never give.
How not quite tasteful the wine; how not quite filling
the bread; how not quite restful the night, how not
quite welcome the dawn. Everything . . . not quite.

My disappointed one, don't expect so much of the
world . . . if it gave you its riches, you still would not
be filled. Always there remains that "not quite." It
is so futile to try to fill up that "not quite." I meant
that to stay distressing; lest you pull up alongside the
road of life, forget you have a road to travel on, and
become content at a "roadside inn." Some things are
reserved for heaven.

I know when you were asking for this and that of
Me that obtaining it would not satisfy. . . . Often
anticipation eclipses the obtainment. I've seen you try
to keep secret your disappointment, but a perceptive
eye could detect a little shadow in your eye where
highlights should be, a little hesitancy in your words of
acclaim, a little slowing down of the heartbeat. I've
seen disappointment in your attaining a position you've
strived long for—it wasn't quite the place in the sun
that you thought it would be. I've seen you disappoint-

ed in friends when their loyalty didn't quite reach. . . .

I want to help you face disappointment. I want you to let it do for your soul what I intended it to do: Lead you to Me—and if ever it seems that I disappoint you, believe that when you see one drop of water, I see the sea. Where you see disappointment, I see an appointment with Me.

ℭ

Doubtful Heart...

Look at a wild rose. It has clasped its petal around a sacred truth: I love you. Look at the autumn milkweed. It is setting free its downiness to proclaim My truth to the four winds: I love you. Look at the night sky; the stars by their own light faintly proclaim: I love you; the moon, willing to depend on another source of light, proclaims it even louder! My mountains reflect My concern with big things; My firefly reflects My interest in tiny things.

I am everywhere as you walk over, under, and around Me, everywhere as you look at Me and through

Me; everywhere as you listen to Me and for Me. But My more approachable presence is in the tabernacle of people. . . . As you bow before My tabernacle in chapel, you ought to bow before one another. Each of you is, or is destined to be, a tabernacle of Me. . . .

In humble adoration you ought to tend to one another's needs, carry one another's burdens, cry one another's tears, smile one another's smiles, and love Me with one another's hearts. Then you can never doubt My love again for it is pouring into you multi-directioned.
ℭ

Despairing Heart...

O, despairing heart—I have said so many things to help you believe I am with you always: "If a man loves Me, he will keep My words, and My Father will love him, and we will come unto him and make our abode with him . . . our home with him, a continual quest within him! I have been standing at the door and I am constantly knocking. If anyone hears Me calling him and opens the door I will come in and fellowship with him and he with Me."

You know that I am an almighty God, and that I can do anything. If you truly believed in My love for you, you would know that My great desire is to be with you always. What is man that I think so much of him? He is an image of Me, created in My likeness. He resembles Me, his Father. My blood is in him—

every time he eats My flesh and drinks My blood, more of My blood courses through him. . . . Eventually My thoughts become his thoughts, he thinks with My understanding, he speaks with My wisdom, and most vital of all, he loves with My love.

I invite you, despairing heart, to hearken to My knock, open unto Me, and let Me fill you with a love that will light up our abode with an everlasting glow and warmth that will dispel every shadow of despair and replace it with living hope. Ours will be a home of love where the hearth is My love for you burning around your love for Me. Will your despair today convince you that you must open the door and let Light light smoldering flax?

Thirsting Heart...

You cry out as you search inside your soul for Me: "My God, my God, why have you abandoned me?" I do not answer. I do not stir. I do not respond in any way to your longing cry. Why? Because I want you to find Me in others.

For so long you found Me sufficiently within. Your eyes grew unaccustomed to seeing others' needs; your ears no longer heard faint but very urgent calls. So I left, that you might search for Me outside yourself. Now, for a while, you won't find Me safely in locked tabernacles, nor in Sacred Scripture behind illumined print. I'm not in pages. I'm in streets. I'm not in quiet, I'm in noise. I'm not tangibly felt within you either— right now.

If you are thirsting for Me, then serve Me by serving others. If the cup from which you drink does not seem to contain "living water," start giving others a drink in My name. Then satisfy your thirst from what is left after serving them and I promise you, it will be "living water." My thirsting heart, stop looking for me where you think that I should be, and begin to look for me where you'd least expect I'd be.

I'm not asking for never-ending prayers, I'm

asking for never-ending love and service in My name.
I'm not expecting you to come to Me alone—but
with a never-ending number of those you gave
"living water" in My name. Then, when I call you to
me, you will not be a single note, a single soul,
but a glorious symphony, a triumphant communion of
souls.

Painful Heart...

Pain can touch your life and create a new dimension of being if you don't fight it, or run from it. Relate it to pain that I suffered on earth.

Compare the throb of your headache to the pulse of pain under the crown of thorns. Compare your backache to the strained, pulled muscles under the weight of the cross. Compare your loneliness and abandonment to the Heart that cried, "Why have you forsaken me?" Compare your infidelity of friends to "Judas, would you betray with a kiss?" Compare your rejection by friends to Peter's "I swear I know him not." Compare your tears of hopelessness to My tears over Jerusalem when I was forced to face the truth, "Thou wouldst not come to Me." Compare the infraction of justice you suffer to "Crucify him, crucify him."

Do not run from pain . . . wait and see what it has to teach you. Let it crush you and see what perfumes arise. Like wheat grains, be crushed to make bread; like red grapes, be crushed to make wine; like rose petals, be crushed to make perfume; like Me, be crushed to serve mankind. . . .

Unfaithful Heart...

So many of you will be My followers when all is going well. . . . You have a holy feeling inside and you find My Spirit embracing you from every scripture page. Then I withdraw my closeness. . . . I must do this to wean you from needing My spiritual comforts. Otherwise, in seeking them, you cease to seek Me.

Now you begin to feel the full weight of the cross. . . . You begin to taste blood and you promptly decide it might be best if you became a little less serious about life . . . a little less serious about following Me. It might be best not to try to know Me too well!

I've sadly watched you take another path . . . anything to get away from Me.

If you would not follow Me, then I must follow you . . . through the mountains, valleys, rivers, fields, cities, until you come to the awesome truth that *I* am the Way, the Truth, and the Life! I am the Good Shepherd, sorrowing heart. One by one, I call My sheep, one by one they answer Me. I am calling . . . you have not answered, but a Good Shepherd never stops calling . . . and hoping.

Self-Willed Heart...

Clouds hover, smothering out the distant starlights. The world is encased in a tomb of darkness. There is no looking out, there is no looking in . . . only a tractless void. This is how it is to be imprisoned in a self-willed heart.

"O God," you cry out through the muffled stillness, "roll back the darkness; rise up, be my Dawn." Then, watch the dawn. See what I will do for you— relax in the darkness, accustom your eyes to the absence of light. Then watch the brightening haze that begins to outline the horizon. It is disclosing the highway of your pilgrimage to Me . . . from self to Me! Obscure at first, but gradually becoming more and more distinct.

Note the bold, red strokes of progressing dawn . . . bloodred pangs, stabs like knives that are painfully striking you free . . . now less red, as gold conquers; the gold is winning, triumphantly victorious! My whole world is open to you! I am your dawn, your noonday sun, your setting sun! Rise with Me in the east, reign with Me at the noonday zenith, gently descend with Me to the western horizon. Let your will be made molten in the rays of Me so that it will never be able to entomb you in its rigidity. Molten liquid . . . so that you may pass freely; others may enter that you might expand freely! I will provide the temperatures to keep you molten. Rise with Me each day. . . .

Limp Heart...

I can do most for your sanctification when you become limp in My hands—when you are willing to loosen your grip on what has been your spiritual scaffolding for all these years; when you are willing to have the only sure ground you know pulled out from under you; when your hands have relinquished everything—even the hand of your last friend; when your heart has let go of all it was sure it couldn't survive without; when you are willing to let your mind change on anything I prompt; when you are willing to bare yourself to any instrument I must use—loneliness, rejection, failure, poor health, injustice, discrimination—then, limp-in-My-hands heart, I will recreate you!

But expect this, most willing heart . . . others will have friends; you, not. Others will be praised; you, forgotten. Others will find consolation; you, emptiness. Others will find love; you, rejection. Others' faults will be overlooked; yours, magnified.

But loving, limp soul, if you are willing to suffer all this, I will make you holy. I will do more—I will transform all that you suffer for Me into such unspeakable joy that the only suffering you will ever know again, will be not to suffer. "Come, take up your cross, and follow me. . . ."

Freed Heart...

Free heart, I give you today! Leap from mountaintop to mountaintop, skip from valley to valley taking My love to everyone you meet. My people are needy people. Each of them needs something—love, attention, care, money. If the need is not apparent ask them, "What do you need from me?"—then give. I cannot answer your prayers for them unless you are willing to sacrifice for them. I cannot answer your prayers for a hungry man, if you yourself will not feed him; I cannot answer your prayers for a suffering soul if you won't suffer with him.

It is so easy to say, "I'll pray for you," when it's your love, your time, your helping hand, your money that they need. It is so easy to say, "I understand," when all we mean is "I'm glad this trial is yours, not mine." It's so easy to say, "Trust in God," when it's your strength they need; so easy to pick them up, but so hard to keep walking with them; so easy to give advice, but so hard to listen to their deep inner pleadings. You are freed . . . freed to love, to give, to understand—use your freedom to set My captives free! ℭ

Lonely Heart...

I said, "It is not good for man to be alone." Yet, oh so many times I pull your friends from you, and you are painfully alone. Even surrounded by friends, you are an island and can only be talked to from distant shores. How often I have witnessed your heart crying, "Oh friend, I cannot hold you close enough; you are still so very far away from me."

That excruciating gap you must always sense, yet you are everlastingly trying to span it. You have learned that no arms will reach. I planted within you a homesickness for Me. I did this to keep you striving for Me. So many of you will exhaust yourselves trying to extinguish this flame of yearning with other hopeful fulfillments, while I stand by and watch you pass Me by.

Lonely heart, stop running, stop searching. Recognize the aloneness you feel, look at it truthfully, honestly, and courageously and lovingly. Admit your hopelessness in alleviating it. Recognize your inability to escape it. Then, in hope, not despair, lift that lonely heart to Me. Sometimes I will fill it with friends; sometimes, with Me; sometimes, only with the full understanding that I know and understand; sometimes with not even that assurance. Sometimes I will fill it with My absence.

Your inner being may passionately crave the heart of a fellow human being to talk to, to understand, and I may not grant what you ask. But I will give you the understanding of faith to believe that I'm aware of your loneliness, knowing that it is not time to dry your tears. Sometimes time must evaporate them. If a friend were to wipe them away too soon, you might not grow as I have planned for you.

Let My awareness of what you suffer now in lone- liness be your companion. Offer it to Me. . . . I can use it to shape you! You, watch with Me in Gethsemane . . . let the others sleep. With Me, understand loneliness; with Me, listen; with Me, be healed.   ℭ

Broken Heart...

Loving heart, every pulsation of your heart courses My blood and yours throughout your body. Sadly I have watched some of this precious nourishment ebb away because there is a break in your heart.

You kept your heart so openly vulnerable, so unguarded, so woundable to everyone. Then, not an alien, not a stranger, but your closest friend broke it. Not keenly and swiftly with words, but joggedly and slowly with unexplained indifference.

Weakened by the loss of blood, you realized more than ever your dependence on Me. The more you called, the richer became My transfusions to you. Now that more of My blood than yours flows through you, I want to heal that broken heart—the blood that is dwindling from the break could nourish other souls rather than aimlessly river through the sands of time.

In My eternal now, I reach back and instantly heal the break. You are serving My purposes without knowing it, by responding to My healing touch and believing that your world is unfolding according to My universal plans. There may remain in your heart that "why, why" that began so many years ago when your fragile, open heart was broken. But with that incessant "why" will come the understanding that "all things work together unto good for those who truly love Me."

When you see what the loving willingness to remain in painful darkness until My light lets you see the "why," you will say, "Break my heart, again, and again, and again. The more of Your blood that You transfuse, the more I become You—and the less I remain me. I can bear the 'why' and take comfort in your one noncommittal response! Just because!"

℃

Fearful Heart...

The grass is here today, withered tonight, and cast away to be burned tomorrow. Yet if I so adorn the grasses of the field which are here today and gone tomorrow, how much more I think of you who live forever!

Yet, you do not look to Me for sustenance, you live as if all solutions to life had to be found within your intellect. Methodically you plan your solutions, but I *am* the solution. You seek companionship, but I am the *Companion*. You seek food and I am the only Bread that fills. You seek clothing and I am the only *Mantle* that covers and warms. You worry into tomorrow and I told you, "My grace is sufficient"—for *today*. I give you your *daily* bread—but fearfully you reach for tomorrow's too. . . .

Fearful heart, please believe that I have your tomorrow in My heart. Your needs will be supplied but I want you to look to Me for your needs, and not in a storehouse where lack of faith has piled up provisions. You strive for position, then arriving, you are constantly distressed over holding it; you discover a pearl of considerable price and watch fearfully lest someone pull it from you. You cling tightly to a friend's hand in constant wariness over someone else winning him from you. You fear a stormy sky; you fear a scorching sun; you fear the shadows that keep you from seeing clearly, you fear the brightness that makes you see too clearly.

Fearful heart, lay the quiverings that fear initiates in My heart and as I once calmed the sea's waves, I'll still your heart waves. ❤

Jealous Heart...

I have given many gifts to many people. My garden of humanity thrills the eye with exciting diversity and my Spirit blowing through wafts a multi-perfumed wind to the world. The clover gently blends with the new-mown hay and together they praise Me. The bleat of the lamb and the neigh of the horse blend into a harmony and together they praise Me.

If the clover were jealous of the new-mown hay, I would not receive a blend of praise. If the lamb said, "I cannot compete with the strong voice of the horse," I would not receive a blend of praise. So, too, jealous heart, if you refuse to sing Alleluia with a more gifted voice than yours, I will miss that blend that I was meant to hear. Do not look upon the accomplishments of others as if they were reminders of your inadequacies. Rejoice with your brother, make the hosannas ring, for another event of the universe has unfolded according to My plan.

I don't want notes, I want chords; I don't want solos, I want choirs; I don't want a drummer, I want drummers. Be content with the gifts that you have been given. Praise Me with them. Do not judge the gifts of others. Do you know what it cost the grape to now be wine, what it cost the wheat to now be bread; what it cost the sinner to now be saint?

Let us look within ourselves and see what raw material is still there to work with and see if that little strain of melody could become a symphony, if that fragile little word could become an everlasting Alleluia!

Loving Heart...

Will you be the one who will serve Me intensely? Will you listen to the heart cries of your neighbor after everyone else has walked away . . . will you be the one who stays up longest to hear his woeful story? Will you be the one to look longest for some trace of Me in the desolate, the derelict, the alcoholic? Will you try to find some resemblance of the Father in the one who slanders you? Will you be the one to keep on loving even when the love is unrequited? Will you ask others in to share your meal when there is no assurance of your next meal? Will you go forth and console others when your own need of consolation is beyond tears? Will you forgive others even though others refuse to forgive you? Care, when no one cares; love, when no one loves; fill others from your own emptiness?

Could you rather pardon than be pardoned; could you rather like than be liked; love, rather than be loved? Understand, rather than be understood? Can you accept insult, and give forth praise in exchange . . . take ridicule and give forth understanding in exchange? Will you listen attentively even though your own problems are thundering in your heart? Will you speak lovingly of My will even when it has crushed you? Then, surrendered heart, minister to My people in pure love.

Possessive Heart...

"O God," you cried to Me, "give me just one person
who will love me as I love him. You give me a friend,
my heart is filled with greatest expectations—but
soon I find the friend is no longer running with me . . .
he's stopped, conservatively, along the roadside.
Come, I beckon. But he is no longer interested.

"I will search the highways and the byways and I
will not cease my searching until I find someone who
will run all the way to You with me . . . one who will
not count the costs, will not stop to bind up wounds,
will not ever say no to love's endless demands."

I've heard your cry, and I'm giving you someone
in whom your expectations will meet sublime heights:
My Son. He will run with you all the way. He will keep

you breathless tending to the many needs of My people as you soar through life. He will help you see what your eyes alone could never discern. He will help you hear what your ears alone could never detect. He will help you touch hearts which your hand alone could never do. "As the deer that longs for running water," so does your soul long for a friend like Him.

So stop, possessive heart; do not ask to possess a friend—you will possess him, fill him, overpower him, and still long for more to love. You will ask of him what he has no potential to fill. Ask Me for My Son. I gave Him to you in a general way, now take Him in a personal way and *run* hand in hand. ❤

Unloving Heart...

An unloving heart is not a natural heart. A heart is born with a natural proclivity to love. . . . From its first beat to its last it was meant to beat in love. But some hearts never received the needed priming.

What would have flowed so naturally with this needed priming could not leave the heart. Love stopped growing. The unloved heart slowly became an unloving heart. It needed someone to love it, so that it could love in return. We are shaped by those who love us, and even more forcibly shaped by those who refuse to love us.

I want to call you, unloving heart, back to living.
I will pick up the stitches that others let drop; I will
knit you back into wholeness. Some do not want to be
loved by Me because they feel they are unlovable.
They cannot believe that I love them for what they are.
Accepting My love may impose obligations to make
themselves lovable, and they would rather remain in
apathetic unlovableness. I'm not asking in return from
you right now other than that you let My love into
your heart, not questioning My love or your worth-
iness. Primed with My love, yours will flow. . . .

Resentful Heart...

O resentful heart, stop, do not come to My altar imprisoned in revenge, but turn around, go to the one for whom you feel such strong adverse feelings. Tell him that with My help the seething waters can be cooled.

As it is now wave begets deeper wave and the surging gives your heart no rest, day or night. Memory of the hurting experience rips the sky like a steel knife blade and following rumbles the thunder of a continuing and intensifying revenge.

You are not free, resentful heart. You feed on your ill feelings and are nourished with slow death. Your tumultuous heart can no longer thrive on wholesome thoughts for revenging weeds have choked them out. You say, I was not the cause of the mishap. I understand, and still I am asking you to turn the other cheek—if that receives a blow at My request to offer it, it is still better for your cheek to sting than for your heart to be eaten away by the acrid acid of resentment.

Resentful heart, you *bind* My hands when you pray, "forgive me my trespasses, as I forgive those who trespass against me." *As* you forgive . . . and you do not forgive? My forgiveness to you is chained. I see

44

you engulfed in the clouds of unforgiveness and I
know that the wild rose you stepped on you didn't see
. . . the child you brushed by you didn't hear, the
handshake you just gave you didn't feel. . . . Brilliant
sunrises don't rise in your heart, peaceful sunsets
don't descend in your heart.

In your heart now, say with Me, "I want the
disturbing waves of resentful unrest to be stilled as I
say with My Heavenly Father: 'Peace, be still.' " ℃

Anxious Heart...

"Look at the lilies . . . they neither spin nor toil, yet behold their beauty! The birds of the air, neither sowing nor harvesting, yet provided for. . . ." Then you, oh fearful heart, why are you so troubled that you walk right by my lilies missing beauty and walk right through my covey of birds missing melody?

You aren't hearing my invitations. "Come to me, I will give you rest; ask Me, and I will hear you, talk to Me, I will understand; cry, and I will know the reason for every tear." Let the penetrating rays of My love shatter the anxiety that strangles you. Let My love set you free! Free to see that you need not carry your worry, free to see that it can be made My concern, free to understand the full impact of My words. "Seek Me first, and all else will be given unto you."

Oh, my anxiety-filled heart, how could you worry ever if you fully believed this? Do you believe that I hurled the stars into the heavens? Then believe that I can hurl highlights into your troubled eyes! Do you believe that I lifted the earth into its designed place? Then believe that I can lift all that fills your anxious heart this moment and put it into the furnace of My heart so that all that remains is love! Perfect love casts out all fears.

Put Me first, and jubilantly watch all the things that seem so wearisome right now fade into oblivion. Soon you may wonder what it was that weighed on your heart. Do you believe that I can bring you to such a state of blissful forgetfulness? Let My blazing love for you sear your heart, brand it forever with these words: "Seek Me . . . all else will be given . . . given in measure beyond expectation . . . given through love without measure."

Overburdened Heart...

My providence is all pervasive. I was up before today dawned. I have seen everything that has happened to you today. Not a sparrow can fall to the ground without My knowing it. Knowing this and believing this, why can't you put your life into My hands? Why is it so hard for you to let go of all your problems? Why do you feel that you must go doggedly on shouldering the whole weight? . . .

Since I have given you free will, I cannot pry your clenched hands open and steal your burdens from you.

You must hand them willingly to Me. My hands are already placed around yours to receive. I'm watching for the slightest sign of relaxing muscles showing Me you are ready to release what is so heavy to hold.

"My burden is light" . . . but only when you've shared it with Me. "My yoke is easy" . . . but only when it lays over My shoulder too. I said, "I will give you rest" but I first said, "Come to Me. . . ." Over-burdened heart, take just one heavy step toward Me— it will be your *only* heavy step.

Dying Heart...

    You awaken each day and face the sun—but one
of these days, it is going to be the Son of God!
As the sun reaches widespread over the heavens,
so I will sweep you into My presence and you will be
able for the first time to look straight into the sun,
the Son of God! No darkness will be left anywhere—
as My face shines forth like a light in the temple!
No silence will be left anywhere as My voice issues
forth and resounds through the temple.

    Then *your* life will be shouted from the housetop.
. . . All the good you have done and forgotten about;
all the good you should have done and have forgotten
about. Those you have helped bring to Me will sing
hosanna to *your* name, those you were indifferent
toward will surround you in silence. Every drink of

cold water given in My name will merit its reward now. As you measured out your love and concern for others, so it shall be measured out to you now. You fed Me when you fed mine; you clothed Me when you clothed mine; you comforted Me when you comforted mine.

Now I, your heavenly Father, will feed you at My banquet table, will clothe you in My robe of glory, will comfort you with My continual presence. Travel-weary now, you are nearing Me. I stand, open-armed, ready to receive you in the place I prepared for you the very moment my love conceived you. Come, not with hesitant step, but with the confident step of a prodigal son who sees the light in the window of his home—welcoming him in from the night.

Rejected Heart...

How many times I have seen you, heart full of love, trying to give it away . . . love, the most precious balm that mankind so sorely needs! You, extravagant enough to upturn the whole heart full, return from your quest, heart still brimming over with the love that no one seemed to want from you. What can you do with your love . . . can it wait endlessly to be received? Will it evaporate with time . . . will it lose its fragrance?

Yes, so expend it lavishly. Let it spill, let the thirsty ground drink its perfumed liquidness. Let the winds be fragranced by it if you can find no heart that will open to it. You, the giver, the bestower, will be the receiver and it does not depend on the reception your gift of love receives. Unrequited love merits My reward. You saw My love unrequited. But I never withdrew it. I ask you not to withdraw yours either. All the times you are turned away, you will be returning to Me. I am there in your every rejection. I am the home to which you return each nightfall. Every time you try to give a "cup of cold water in My name" and your helpfulness is positively refused I will drink the water in *your* name.

Prepare yourself to be rejected, but see beyond
the rejection to Me, for I am there. I said, "Whatsoever
you do the least of My brothers, that you do to Me."
When they throw that cup of love, or that cup of water
back at you, I feel it, too. It hurts Me to see your heart
so full it must exclaim, "Lord, give me someone to
love!" Someone to expend my love on, someone to
pour perfumed oil on. . . .   ℭ

Missionary Heart...

"Go forth and teach all nations" about Me.
If they knew how empty their lives were and how full
their lives could be, they would receive you with open
arms and empty cups. But as it is, they have filled
their cups with substitutions for Me. The substitutions
are far from satisfying, but they are better they think
than an empty cup. Therefore your commission to
spread the news of My love is a difficult overture.

First, you have to convince My people that what they have in their cups ought to be overturned and spilled out, emptied in order that *they* might be filled with "new wine, living water." Then you must tell them of My infinite love for them, with My words, My life, your words, and most important of all, your life. If you can do this, My missionary heart, you will draw many souls to Me . . . and the cups will be running over with the new wine of Me.

Insecure Heart...

"O God," you cry out to Me, "I feel so unbe-
longing. I've tried to fit in, tried to be one of the many.
But I'm always on the outside looking in. I hear the
music, but I know it's not being played for me."

Come, fearful one, follow Me. I call you to become
a fisher of men! Others will answer your call, for you
will be calling with My voice. Others will respond to
your love, for you will be loving with My love. . . .
Sparks from your love will fly off and enkindle others.
Your heart alone cannot enkindle fire of such intensity,
but let Me touch it with mine and it will shout with
leaping flames.

First, you must come close enough to Me to be
enkindled with My love. Make Me your first concern.
Do not care about how you belong, how you fit in with
the world. Place this insecurity that you suffer in My
heart. It will burn away in the furnace of My heart,
leaving you with a security that will enable you to
hear the music, and not care at all that it is not being
played for you—for it will be My promptings that will
be important to you.

Others will be drawn to you like a magnet . . .
they will be fed by you and they will notice how

nourishing the food! They will come to your banquet, and they will never tire of your menu. It will be living water that you supply—for I am supplying you—and because you forgot yourself, your insecurity, your not belonging, and dedicated your tremblingly insecure heart to Me! You will be so busy, so concerned with serving other insecure hearts, that one day you will discover most unexpectedly that you are secure with Me; secure with My people.

Seek Me, and all else will be added unto you. "For I am the Lord your God who upholds your right hand, who says to you, 'Do not fear, I will help you'" (Isaiah 41:13).

Unbelieving Heart...

When you unfold a rosebud and see how gracefully it clasps its heart-secret, don't you begin to think that maybe I exist? As the straightway of the pine points to Me all day and night aren't you tempted to look up at the object of its pointing? As the sunflower devotedly turns to face its god-sun all day, closing its openness to everything when its god is gone, don't you long for something that pervasive to believe in?

When death stealthily takes away a beloved friend don't you wish you had someone to blame it on? To whom do you direct your grief? Is life so satisfying for you that you don't need a Distant Goal to direct your life forward? Is today reason enough for today? Is today just a separate entity that doesn't need to fit in with a series of days that lead on to one Last-Most-Meaningful-Day? Does it give you a vagabond worthlessness to feel that today's events are unrecorded and will pass into oblivion with neither acknowledgment, reward, nor reprimand? Is it a natural proclivity to do good all day and know the goodness will not resound through the halls of a grateful Lord's mansion for all eternity?

Man, like grass, here today, gone tomorrow—and

forgotten forever: Many have thought this: "If there were not a God, I would have to invent one." You, whose soul was created for one purpose—Me—refuse to believe in Me. "O Jerusalem—how often I would have gathered you as a hen gathers her chicks to her . . . but thou wouldst not." Will you go into eternity never knowing why you were born?

O unbelieving heart, let me show you in a thousand ways that I am real. Sometimes the price of free will bankrupts Me. . . .

Lost Heart...

Lost heart, will you forever go through life not sure of your place in My divine orderings of the universe? I want you to feel right to be serving where you are serving now. I need you to fill your position— no one else will do! When in that moment of over- flowing love that I conceived you, I knew what position I wanted you to play in My world symphony of man- kind. It seems you have not understood how important it is for you to serve Me where I have assigned you.

You keep straining to detect new directions—your eye is ever vigilant, scanning the horizon for other possibilities of serving Me. You are forever questioning —hesitant and insecure lest you miss My calling. Serve in full confidence where you are now. If I wish to relocate you, the call will be vigorous and full. If I want you to grasp opportunities as they present themselves I will speak to your soul in ample time and decisiveness. My answers for you will come in peace and surety. If you are indecisive or confused, you will know it is not I that speaks.

Wait upon Me in complete confidence and trust. I will take your hand in mine and gently lead. I have the blueprint of you that I had planned from the beginning of time. You were on My mind when I threw the heavens into course. You are forever on My mind.

So, lost heart, find yourself in Me. Say with St. Paul, "I grasp ever more purposefully that purpose for which Christ grasped me—namely, to recognize ever more clearly my responsibility to God and to man. To commit myself fully to God's purpose in this broken humanity."

World Heart...

Lulled as an infant to the world's restless music you don't hear the symphony in the pines. Screamed at by neon lights, you haven't seen the quiet Milky Way. Shod against rough sidewalks, you haven't felt the cool wetness of the meadow grass. Shouted at by loud discotheques, you haven't heard the sustained Alleluia from the church organ. Urged on by practical business you have banked your material wealth daily, and your spiritual wealth annually. Lured by advertisement, you have massed trinkets and scoffed at self-denial.

You have tripped over the common man in your

frenzied run to the influential. You have pushed away the lowly to serve the superficial needs of the mighty. You have found your place in the sun and are completely unaware of how many shiver in the shade. You think you have found Me, and you are little concerned about the countless who have not.

Your life has slowly lost its spiritual pitch and you are unaware of being out of tune with Me; you wonder at the discord, but search *outside* of yourself for the discordance. World heart, let me give you the correct pitch once again and let's make the melody harmonious *and* divine.

Indifferent Heart...

I sent My love to you today in many ways. Through a friend's tear, through a child's warm hand, through an old woman's need of your smile, but your indifferent heart didn't recognize Me . . . didn't feel it had been touched.

I could not get through the impregnable fortress you have built around yourself. You can no longer feel My touch—or My needy people's touch.

You are safe from us—you are safe from hearing the mournful cries of the lonely, but you are also missing the meadowlark. You are safe from seeing the tears of the neglected child, but you are also missing the scintillating waterfall. You are safe from feeling the wet, feverish hand of a despairing soul, but you are missing the warmth of the hand that trusts you. True, it is painful to care; but not to care is living death.

Awaken to a new resurrection . . . reach out, let the warmth in My hand raise your temperature, melt down the indifference, and lay you open to the deepest joy—and the deepest suffering.

Talking Heart...

Never-silent heart, let Me heal you of the need
to be ever talking. I understand your desperate need
to feel accepted and respected, therefore I understand
your self-revealing words. I understand your need to
communicate with others, so I understand how your
words burst from you in hapless disarray. I understand
your crying need to be understood, so I understand
your talkative quest for just the right person to lay
open your noisy heart.

I want to teach you to silence your heart. Dwell
on the silent spaces between rain-drenched rose
petals, dwell on the silent still space between mountain-
tops, dwell on the silent space between friends who've
learned the communicative powers of silence. Dwell

on the silence between you and Me when prayer words won't come. . . . Realize that words are only one means of communication. Don't feel awkward in silence with Me, or with your friends. A glance, a sigh, a touch . . . let them speak. Instead of using words first use them only when other means of communication are down.

In the silence you will learn to sift the chaff from the grain . . . and then what you speak after this sifting process of silence will have more import and impact and will be less and less in quantity and more and more in quality. Let me heal you of your incessant need for words. When you are attuned to my silence, you will understand things beyond the reach of words.

ℭ

Vain Heart...

You have looked inward too long, vain heart. Your vision has become very shortsighted. You can see only as there is something in it for you. And the periphery is closing in.

If you let Me apply my eternal vision of you, I will lengthen and widen your vision way beyond the immediate; a whole new world opens to you! Now you are indeed imprisoned because you apply, consciously or subconsciously, the question: "What's in it for me?" How you restrict your heart, your world!

Let Me help you see others; let Me help you draw others into your world; let Me help you see their tears, see their despair, their resentments, their slavery. How can you grow when your gaze is forever inward? Focus way out . . . see that most distant person on your horizon . . . a stranger, and a situation with surely "nothing in it for you." Focus until your eyes become adjusted to his needs—I will be helping you to forget yourself.

"He who would save his life, will lose it; he who loses his life for me, will save it." Let my healing sight correct your vision. When I see you again focusing inward I will put another person on that distant horizon. I will keep the action of your sight from becoming centrifugal. I will spin it outward until you can detect needs from a continually lengthening distance. You cannot remain a vacuum. If you will not be filled with others, you will be filled with yourself. When you are filled with others, I can come in with them unnoticed. But if you are filled with self, there is no password for Me. Self will become a more and more demanding tyrant, and you will become more and more enslaved, less and less free, and deeper and deeper locked in a prison of self.

Let me show you distant horizons instead! Keep focusing on the distant horizon. Someone, near or far, will be in your line of vision.

Restless Heart...

"Peace, be still" and the sea closed its countless whitecapped mouths. Let My "Peace, be still" calm that restless surging heart of yours. Offer your restless state to Me. The winds will calm, and the waves that beat up against your heart will be subdued.

Collapse into My arms and bring to rest your restlessness in Me. I want to hold your heart still so it does not exhaust itself in ceaseless, purposeless activity. Let the light of My understanding enlighten you so it becomes clear to you why you are restless. If you are restless to rest in Me, that is to be expected. You were created to live in Me and nothing will still that eternal longing but possession of Me. But the restlessness that I see in you is a result of your not understanding that eternal longing in you. You are trying to satisfy something spiritual with something material, and in that, you are born to lose.

"If only I can attain this, then I will be content," you have said countless times to your surging heart. After attaining it, your hands are empty, and so is your heart; pitching waves within send echoes into your empty life.

Peace, be still, ever-moving heart. Recognize now that your greatest need is Me. Set your heart's sail on

Me, expect that waves will attack and endanger your craft as you travel life's seas, but keep your eyes ever fixed on Me. The roar of the seas will be silenced, the salt spray of distraction will lose its sting, you will learn to trust the Gentle Wind that guides . . . lift anchor; listen for My direction . . . trust that I understand your restlessness; and trust that I can lead you to restful waters. ℭ

Self-Important Heart...

O self-important heart, your desire to be first in all things keeps you rapacious and restless. You must be first in the race for everything; you must be first in the heart of everyone. Let me heal you of this need to excel. . . .

Forget loftiness: Be reborn in a stable. Forget fame: Live 30 years in complete obscurity. Forget popularity: Listen to "Give us, Barabbas!" Forget justice: Listen to "Crucify, crucify!" Forget dignity: Die ignobly on

Mount Calvary. I took the last place. I came to serve, not to be served.

O heart, so weary of trying so hard to be important, let me rearrange your values. . . . Seek to be first with Me; this will require that you seek to be last in everything you do. The last to be thanked, the last to be appreciated; the last to be called friend. But be consoled with these words: "The last shall be first . . . in My kingdom."

Impoverished Heart...

In your world of mortar and concrete what is there to nourish your heart? What is there to put you in touch with the Eternal? The faded store signs, the cracking sidewalks, the weatherworn storefronts, the faulty-functioning neon signs all point to decadence and mortality.

When the psalmist sang, "He leads me by the restful waters, in verdant pastures He gives me rest," he realized the value of replenishing the impoverished heart. With no replenishment of spirit, the heart slowly loses the pitch—so gradually that it is unaware that it is no longer at concert pitch. The heart settles for a life far beneath the lofty goals it once had. Dreams return often enough for the heart to say, "Oh, what might have been!" And could still be!

If your happiness depends on what the world can give you, it will be shallow. It can lead you to the heights only as long as the music continues and the dance goes on. If your happiness depends on what I can give you, it will be enduring. I give you My rolling hills and deep valleys to teach you to live on the heights and the depths. I give you My sun and My clouds to teach you to live in happiness and sorrow. I give you My symphony of pines and My eternal silence to teach you to live in loudness and stillness. I give you My presence and My absence to teach you to live with Me. $\heartsuit$

Exhausted Heart...

Tired, weary heart, how often you ask me for strength. Can you believe that maybe your weakened state serves me better right now?

As I said to St. Paul: "I am with you. That is all you need. My power shows up best in weak people." Say now with St. Paul: "Now I am glad to boast about how weak I am. I am glad to be a living demonstration of Christ's instead of showing off my own power and abilities."

If you are strong, let your strength serve Me; if you are weak, let your weakness serve Me. There is no state of your being that cannot be used to serve Me—except sin. Serve Me in your confusion, serve Me in your aloneness: Serve Me in your incompleteness. If you think your weary heart cannot initiate another heartbeat, let that last heartbeat be for Me. . . . "If any man will lose his life for Me, he will gain it!"

So if you have lived today for Me and are exhausted now, glory in that exhaustion! When others would have said, "Lord, I'm too hungry to go on without food," you did. When others would have said, "Lord, I'm too thirsty," you went on. When others would have ignored any delay in getting home, you heard your brother's call of distress and tended to his needs.

You who have kept such a sensitive watch on My inspirations to you, lift up, send up, your frail Amen on this day of service to Me and My heavenly choirs will magnify it to fill the heavens with hosannas! **C**

Forgotten Heart...

Learn to include Me intimately in your life. Learn to believe that I care intimately about you. Nothing you have on your mind is too insignificant to share with Me. No problem you have to solve is too difficult for Me.

I am waiting every moment for you to tell Me more about yourself. I want to be intricately interwoven into the tapestry of you. You may feel forgotten by others, but you must never feel forgotten by Me. Because you can be so confident of My love for you, you can comfort others.

Unlike the sea which reflects the sky it faces, many times you must reflect the opposite of what you see in My people. When you see restlessness, reflect

peace; seeing despair, reflect hope; seeing faithless-
ness, reflect faith; seeing a lack of Me, reflect the fullness of Me. Like a sensitive photographic paper, you
must be sensitive to the reflections that people's needs
cast. Like a sensitive photographic negative, you must
be able to reverse what you see.

I will give you the discernment to understand the
needs of others, confident that you will be My instrument. In the scurry of being so very used by Me, you
will not feel forgotten. You will be caught up in the
excitement of seeing the forgotten brought into the
human circuit once again . . . a human circuit that
will light up into one glorious hosanna someday.

Insensitive Heart...

Because you have shuddered with pain the world inflicts, you have hardened the casing of your heart. It takes a great force now to pierce that protection. But is this insured protection a satisfying state? Are you happy feeling nothing?

Each of the outside stimuli that come to man has a purpose. There is nothing unordained in My universe. Sorrow says, "Let me come in awhile." You hardly felt the call, and barred your heart door more securely. Joy said, "Let me in awhile." But there may be prices to pay, you say to yourself—and prefer to keep that heart door locked. Wary of all, you exclude all.

Your brother is right outside your heart's door but your insensitive ears don't pick up fragile calling voices anymore. . . . Your insensitive eyes don't see the overwhelming human needs teeming all around you. You are safe now, insensitive heart. So safe—and so empty, so safely empty. What satisfactions do you find in your impenetrable world? What joys do you find in safeguarding self? Self is an insatiable master to serve— growing, ever-growing in its demands.

At first, just open the windows of your soul—those foreign sounds you hear are My people expressing their

need for you—the expressions on their faces are expressions of need! Let me crack the exterior of your
encased heart—become vulnerable once again! The
sounds will be deafening at first and it will take time to
single out a voice: the scenes you witness will be
overwhelming at first and it will take time to single
out a need you can best satisfy. But as you become
attuned to need, when your vision is refocused on the
needs of others—you'll see Me through the fragile
vessel of them.

Just look from the windows of your heart—still
secure behind the locked door. Soon, I know you will
open your heart door—everlastingly wide!

Tempted Heart...

O heart, so tempted, remember that you must live with *you* all day, all night. If you let yourself be led into doing wrong, your heart becomes a bloody battlefield. Not at peace with yourself any longer, the battlefield extends to the whole world . . . world-wide war. The meadowlark's soft song is now a shrieking voice of accusation. Even the wild lily seems to close its petals and not want to share its beauty with you. But the greatest pain of all is your sense of being cut off from humanity, cut off from the Vine, a dead, useless branch that pulls down the living branches and makes them support your dead weight.

The greatest tragedy of all, you grow accustomed

to this crippled state of being, accustomed to sin, and
you are unaware that you, the branch, have become
yellow, dry and about to break off completely from the
Vine. . . . So close to the Source of life, but severed
from it by sin.

All that is necessary to be rejoined is a contrite
heart. I make forgiveness so enjoyable for man that he
is able to say: "Oh happy fault that led me to seek
God's loving forgiveness and understand His deep
love for me." Show Me a contrite heart . . . and I'll
show you how quickly I can nourish a drying branch
into vibrant life! I am the Vine, you are the branches.

♡

Praying Heart...

There is a mellow glow from My tabernacle over you as you kneel here before Me. You just brought your heart here to be exposed to My love. Each quiet, restful beat of your heart brings it closer to mine. . . . This quiet beating is like incense rising, lifting, spiraling to Me.

I like you quiet here before Me—not here to ask Me favors, not here to have Me dry away tears, not here for Me to lift burdens; just here to be here. Just here to let our presences intermingle, just here to let our wills focus into one; just here to love the stillness of both of us—just here to experience trust.

If I am weary I may rest on your peacefulness; if you are weary, you may rest on mine. If I am wounded by indifference to Me, I can be comforted by your special interest in Me; if I am hurt by man's interest in My gifts rather than Me, I can be comforted in your complete satisfaction with My presence—being here wanting nothing.

I will make your face radiant and glowing so others will ask, "Where have you been, what fire has touched your face?" They will run from the chill of the world to the warmth of the Hearth that warmed you. . . . Bring them in and *you* stay, too.

Complex Heart...

Your heart is whipped and whitecapped and I cannot see My reflection in its turbid waters. I cannot say, "Peace, be still" from the outside. You must invite Me into that complex heart so that I can calm it from the inside. I must convince you that the forces you have let in can only keep it in restlessness. You cannot serve so many forces, so many masters.

One moon pulls ebb tides and full tides—what confusion in the waters if I added just one more force, one more moon. How many forces, how many moons are in your sky? The force to be accepted is a very bright moon of yours and causes many high waves. The force to appear successful whips your sea into turmoil. The force to excel, the force for attention; the force to satisfy pride, vanity, self-love. . . . Oh, so many moons in your sky!

If you let Me, I will take all these moons that pull in every direction, combine them into one great light—the light to love Me first—and all other loves will be made into stars. Stars that exist but do not have the power to pull tides, to pull your heart seas asunder. "Seek Me first, and all things will be added unto you." Let Me, as one moon, direct the tides of your heart, rhythmically and serenely, and the stars will take their proper positions of importance. ℭ

Abandoned Heart...

I sheltered you as a hand cups itself over a wind-threatened flame. I kept My all-embracing arms around you. You feared nothing because I cushioned all the hurt you could ever encounter.

Then once I left you alone; you never knew sorrow until then. You called My name, your soul tossed like driftwood in angry waters. "My God, what have I done that you have abandoned me so . . ." you cried. "It is better for you that I leave," I told you. "My absence will teach you more than My presence." You wilted beneath these words crying, "No, no, you can't abandon me. You led me so close to you that I cannot turn back. The world holds nothing for me." And I had to stand by and let My dark night of the soul purge you.

I saw you slowly slump, reduced to one phrase: "I cannot go on. Help me!" and in that moment of complete helplessness you felt My absence as deeply as you had once felt My presence. You were now molten metal that I could shape according to My divine plan for you—and when I brought you out from the dark night of the soul you were resplendent silver that caught every reflection of splintered light from Me and became the light that will diffuse and brighten the path for countless others. ᑕ

Chained Heart...

I have set you completely free. . . . If you are again in chains because of one reason or another, I will loose those for you also. Let me cut forever the chains that enslave.

One cannot live in this world long without being treated in a way that begins to chain the heart. The thoughtlessness of others, the directed maliciousness of others, and maybe the most powerful of all, the bleak indifference of others make us captives. If these weights are not lifted from you, you cannot travel lightly in love with mankind. If this onerous burden is not taken from you, small stimulations may cause you to overact and begin less and less to understand yourself. You will wonder why such small provocation led you to respond so vehemently.

Let My healing light in. These growths nourished by the darkness will succumb to the sunshine of Me, wither, and disappear. They are all in My Eternal Now, and I can handle them as if they had just caused your distress now. I can also reach back through all the years of repeated injuries, gather and subject the accumulated weight to the furnace of My heart. What lightness of heart you will experience! That chain, growing link by link with accumulated weight, slows down your lighthearted steps to Me. You walk heavily and ploddingly. I want to set you completely free . . . unweighted and running to Me! ℭ

Scrupulous Heart...

Let My love loose your chains, chains that have you so weighted you can no longer know any freedom of thought. The smallest incident has power to force you to believe that you have offended Me. . . . You weigh, reweigh, remember, as the past moment casts black shadows on the present moment. Your mind becomes a bloody battlefield as you fight on the front lines of defense against self-accusation.

So many times it is easier to surrender to the enemy and say, "I am guilty, guilty, guilty. I cannot defend myself any longer against assault. . . ." The actual combat is thus ended, but the shame of bearing a guilt so doubtfully yours troubles your soul. It seems

to you the war has ended, but the wrong side has won.
Your unworthy eyes cannot lift themselves to Me.

But *do* look up at Me! *See* My mercy. Understand
My understanding of you. Your soul is set upon
pleasing Me. How often I have heard you pray, "Let
me think, do, or say nothing that would offend you,
my God." When you pledge that kind of loyalty to Me,
you will know for certain when you have sinned. You
cannot slip into serious sin unaware. That would
take a full reversal of will. Do not look upon Me as
a harsh judge. I am a loving Father. When you take
your first step toward Me, I am already running toward
you. . . .

Ambitious Heart...

You rode past My waving wheat fields today and you didn't notice Me waving to you in the ripened heads. You didn't hear Me calling you in the pine-scented winds. You had the demands of the day heavy on your mind and heart. . . . They sheltered you from me.

No, I've tried so many ways today to get your attention—but your mind is focused on things that are already deteriorating as you gaze so longingly on them. "Oh, if I only had this, I'd be perfectly happy," you have said time and again. Then, hands full, you see how empty they are. The search goes on—more and more is added to the complexity of your life . . . and less and less to the contentment of your life. You sit amidst the clutter you hauled in around you, still looking for more to amass.

O ambitious heart, slow down your racing beat. Refocus. Look at Me. Seek Me . . . and all else will be added to you. Let Me be the center—relax in that Oneness—and don't reach out for anything else. I'll *hand* it to you—all that you need for a rich, full life. Don't listen to what the world proclaims you need. How misled you will be; you'll be surrounded with a nothingness that will obscure your vision of Me—and each obtainment will crowd you back into yourself. Reduce your life to its lowest common denominator: Me. And those fractions of life that cannot be reduced down to Me cast from you. Be ambitious in serving Me—all else will be added. ℭ

Grasping Heart...

O grasping heart, if only you could sit back and let the world pass you by. Why must you be allured by the gaudy show of color and the raucous calls to come? . . . How will you return? What satisfactions, what happinesses will you have found to accompany your homeward steps? What effect will your pleasant stay of time have on eternity? Did it draw you closer to Me? All the material possessions that your fingers close so tightly over . . . do they lead to Me?

O heart, grasp what will fill your emptied hands; grasp what will fill your emptied soul. If you can see what you are grasping, then you can be sure it is not everlasting. Can you see love, understanding and care? No, these are the eternal values. What does the world grasp . . . money, position, material possessions? And then like in a bad dream, you open your tightly clasped hand, and it unfolds unto nothingness.

Grasping heart, let me teach you to grasp new things. Relax your grip now—let go, one by one, of inordinate desires—reduce your desires, reduce life's clutterings down to the bare essentials. With a light knapsack through life—you are more able to move, to serve, to love! And the more you extricate yourself from life's encumbrances, the more you empty yourself to be filled—with Me! ♡

Sensitive Heart...

Like a taut violin string I have watched you vibrate from the world's touches when most hearts would not even feel they were touched. I have seen the vibrations continue and the pitch of pain continue a lingering note for days. I have seen you try to still the quivering string only to set it into greater motion and give forth an even more mournful strain. I've seen your attempts to loosen the string and become less sensitive, but this brought the melody of your life into cacophony and you tightened it to its created pitch.

I created your sensitivity for I needed someone to detect and interpret for others the delicate nuances of my creation. You thrill to beauty, but pay for it heavily when you are forced to behold what isn't beautiful. You experience peacefulness at enviable heights, but you suffer at discord at depths no one would care to fall to. I want to soothe the wounds you have suffered through your sensitivity, but I want to remind you that it is my special gift to you—though a costly one for you to accept fully.

I can whisper to you and you will hear my promptings, I can touch you ever so lightly, and you will interpret the touch; the slightest change in wind direction you will perceive, and look for my message. Your heart is sensitively soft in My hands—any indentation I make with my shaping fingers will remain and the former state will not reassert itself. You will notice that my winds are perfumed by the heather o'er which they pass and you will refer the fragrance to My Providence.

O sensitive hearts, you are My artists, My poets, My music masters, My lovers of mankind. Soothe the bruised reed with the thought that your sensitivity is an extravagant gift from Me that gives itself over and over again with each transcendent dawn and each unexpected bird's song.

Misunderstood Heart...

You tried to give to others My love. I asked you to do this so many times: "Beloved, love one another." The world is not attuned to My love and when you tried to bestow it, others questioned it. Your heart was so full and with eagerness in the morning sun you ran to distribute it—as a honeybee from flower to flower. But when you returned at sundown, your heart was still full. You found that only those who have walked and talked with God will listen to you—will accept My love.

I was with you all day, misunderstood heart. I remembered My tears over Jerusalem when I saw you unable to interest anyone with My love . . . "Jerusalem, Jerusalem, how often I would have gathered you." I remembered Peter's denial of Me when your close friends denied knowing you because they were embarrassed by your open proclamation of Me. . . .

So you return now, a heart full of love and a world all about you starving from a lack of love. You have been scorned, rebuffed, ignored, ridiculed and abandoned because you tried to feed My people what you know they need. You were willing to reduce yourself to whatever it took to reach My people . . .

but they would not open their hearts to you—and to My love. Your pain at this was great, because you know so well that you had what My people are hungering for—that was My pain when I said from the cross: "I thirst"—for the souls that will forever thirst, within reach of Living Water.

With the sunrise, faithful vessel of My love, go forth again and offer My people Me. ♡

Sleepless Heart...

With the shadowed soft breath of night, let Me wrap you in My dark. Let your tired mind rest in twilight's embrace. Let my night silence day's demands. Let it take the heights and depths of the day and blend them together into pleasant forgetfulness, neutralizing grief with memory of joy. If your disintegrated mind will not let you do this then quietly offer your unrest to Me. Do not fight it— just lift it.

Picture in your mind the angry seas that whipped and snarled with belligerent waves. Toss with these tumultuous waves—let your unrest seethe with them. Then witness them receding. Slowly . . . slowly smoothing out under the weight of My "Peace, be still." Then listen to Me say over and over again "Peace, be still. . . . Peace, be still."

Then in peace tell me what weighs on your heart . . . one thought at a time until you have given them all to Me—then the streams of your heart will not have to carry them as heavy driftwood and sleep will come. If not, do not worry but "watch and pray with Me—I will give rest to your soul."

Guilty Heart...

"Though your sins be as scarlet, I will make them white as snow."

If only you could *really* believe this! A contrite heart, I would never turn away.

Think back into your childhood—let the sunshine of My grace into all the shadows of unforgotten sin. . . . Subject all the guilt-ridden memories to My grace. Put them into My burning heart—a furnace of love— and never again try to pull them out. Believe that My love has burned them—forever!

Try to feel forgiven. . . . Listen to My words of pardon: "Your sins are forgiven. Go in peace!" In peace! That means that you must forgive yourself, too—or there can be no peace. Do not hold on to any sinful misfortune. Subject it immediately to My healing forgiveness so that My love can burn it from your soul. And then believe, believe: *I have forgiven you.*

I don't want you to feel weighted with sin. I was already weighted with every sin of mankind—all is atoned for already. The countless pills that My people must take to sustain them through a day! Why? Because they do not feel forgiven. Guilt has crippled them. It has haunted, obsessed, and distorted hearts.

Whatever you have done, come to Me with a contrite heart and I can lift the clouds that enslaved your heart and once again you will notice that my trees clap and my mountains echo alleluia!

Christian Heart...

Christian heart, are you really Christian? What have you done to set you apart from those who are not Christian? Have you told of My love crowds that will defy you, or do you just speak of Me when you are comfortably surrounded by church members? Have you extended your hand in charity intimately to a brother in need, or just remotely through a collection plate? Have you walked into a destitute home and helped with your own resources My oppressed and deprived? Have you regularly visited the sick and the lonely, or do you just thank Me that you are not one of them?

Oh Christian heart, will I know you by your love? Let Me help you to become more Christlike. Give Me your life. . . . With it, you will serve Me. I will use all of you. I will demand more and more. . . . I will give the grace you need to give, give, give . . . and then, one way or another, I'll demand that you give Me your life. Christian heart, will you take My grace to accomplish this in your life? Then, I take your life. ♡

Christ Heart...

When you awaken in the morning, and your heart immediately asks, "What can I do for you, Lord?" know that you are serving with My heart. When you encounter a friend who slaps one side of your face and you immediately turn the other side to him, know that you are forgiving with My heart.

When you find a stranger who is hungry and you feed him from your own daily portion, know that you are nourishing him through My heart. When you suffer persecution because of Me with joy and gratitude, know that you are responding with My heart.

When friends, position and wealth are taken from you and you say, "Everything I have is yours, Lord," know you are lovingly surrendering to Me with My heart. When you spend hours with distressed souls, know you are caring with My heart. When you can accept suffering as a reward for accepting previous suffering, know you are enlightened by My heart.

On the last day, when I say to you, "Come, blessed of My Father, to the kingdom prepared for you"— know that your heart *is* My heart.